How we communicate

Bobbie Kalman

The In My World Series

Toronto
New York
Crabtree Publishing Company

The In My World Series
Created by Bobbie Kalman

Editor-in-Chief:
Bobbie Kalman

Editor:
Maria Casas

Writing team:
Bobbie Kalman
Maria Casas
Jo-Anna Boutilier
Susan Hughes

Design and mechanicals:
Halina Below

Illustrations:
Title page by Karen Harrison
Pages 4-27 and cover © Mitchell Beazley Publishers 1982
Pages 28-29 by Halina Below
Pages 30-31 by Deborah Drew-Brook-Cormack
© Crabtree Publishing Company 1986

Typesetting:
Jay Tee Graphics Ltd.

Cataloging in Publication Data

Kalman, Bobbie, 1947-
   How we communicate

(The In my world series)
ISBN 0-86505-074-0 (bound)
ISBN 0-86505-096-1 (pbk.)

1. Communication - Juvenile literature. I. Title.
II. Series.

P91.2.K34 1986   j001.51

For Surina and Shama

350 Fifth Avenue
Suite 3308
New York, N.Y. 10118

102 Torbrick Road
Toronto, Ontario
Canada M4J 4Z5

Contents

4   Receiving information from our senses

6   Gestures, sounds, and language

8   Signaling danger

10   Signs everywhere

12   Using maps

14   Books are great!

16   Sending letters

18   Anna's long-distance call

20   Television — a new invention

22   Rainbow's concert

24   News reports

26   An air-traffic-control tower

28   Let's explore . . . Map-making

30   Try this . . . Secret codes

32   Communication dictionary

4

Receiving information from our senses

To *communicate* means to express ourselves so that others can clearly understand us. We are able to communicate in many different ways. We can listen and speak. Most of us can read and write. We also have special tools to help us communicate, such as computers, telephones, and television. However, our five senses of taste, smell, sight, hearing, and touch are our most important communication tools. Through our senses, we receive information about our surroundings.

The Gerards are using their senses as they prepare dinner. They know the vegetables are ripe because of the bright colors. The vegetables feel firm to the touch. They smell fresh and taste crunchy and sweet. The Gerards receive the information from their senses that the food is good to eat.

Picture talk

If there was a fire in the kitchen, how would this information reach the Gerards?
Which of their senses do the Gerards use in preparing dinner?
Take a walk around your neighborhood.
Make a list of all the things you see, hear and smell. Touch some trees, fences, stones, and other objects with interesting textures. Close your eyes and describe how they feel.

HELLO DAG HI BONJOUR HEJ

BUENOS DIAS こんにちは BUONG

6

Gestures, sounds, and language

Animals communicate by using gestures and sounds. Bees do a special dance to show other bees where there is nectar. Cats arch their backs when they want to frighten their enemies. Herring gulls warn other gulls of danger with a call of alarm.

Like animals, people also communicate with gestures and sounds. We use body language to show how we feel. We smile, frown, wave, shrug, hug, and kiss. We laugh, cry, whistle, and clap.

It is our ability to communicate with words, however, that allows us to share our ideas with others. By using language, we can communicate many kinds of information. We can explain our thoughts in great detail.

Not everyone uses the same language to communicate. How many languages can you speak?

Picture talk

Name the ways in which the Kendalls show that they are happy to see their visitors. If you met someone and could not speak his or her language, how else could you communicate your message? Look at the border of this picture. In which languages is the word "hello" written?
Answer: Dag — Dutch; Bonjour — French; Hey — Swedish; Buenos dias — Spanish; こんにちは — Japanese; Buon giorno — Italian; Guten tag — German

7

Signaling danger

"May Day, May Day! Our ship is sinking," the fishermen shout as they prepare to abandon their boat.

The occupants of the lighthouse have seen the distress signal. They are rushing down to rescue the men. The lighthouse attendant across the channel has sent up flares to warn a second boat of the danger ahead.

Signals alert people to a change. A scream is a signal. It is a sound that is not usually part of the surroundings. It sends a message that something is wrong. There are many other signals that we can see and hear. Bells, horns, and whistles are signals. They are sometimes put on floating buoys to warn ships of dangerous spots in the water. Traffic lights are also signals.

We can use our bodies to give signals. When you put up your hand in class, you signal the teacher that you want to speak. When you shout, you signal that you want someone's attention. How do you signal "Hello?"

Picture talk

Which signals were used to attract people's attention in this picture?
What information do signals give? Why do signals only give part of the information?
Which situations are signals best used for?
Write an adventure story using the action in this picture.

Signs everywhere

"Sign, sign, everywhere a sign." Why does this intersection have so many signs? There are street signs, store signs, and signs that show where things are.

Signs help us to communicate by giving us information through pictures or words. Have you ever seen a picture sign outside a store? Look at the ones in this neighborhood. What type of store is under the sign showing: a loaf of bread, a boot, a fish, a pair of glasses? What other picture signs can you see?

Some signs contain *symbols* which stand for places, objects, or instructions. The traffic signs in the border of the picture each communicate one important piece of information using a symbol. The red sign with the white dash means, "Do not enter!" Look at the picture. Where are cars not allowed to enter? Which sign tells us that parking is not allowed? How do you know? Which sign tells us not to turn left?

The cars must circle the island in the middle of the traffic circle. Which sign tells drivers that there is a traffic circle ahead?

Other signs direct us to certain places. Find the sign in this picture which directs us to: a parking lot, first aid, a beach, telephones, washrooms, campgrounds, and the highway. Which of the signs are temporary? Why?

Using maps

The Goldsteins are visiting a castle. They have climbed to the top of the hill to get a view of the park from above. On top of the hill, they find a map of the castle grounds.

A map looks like a picture of an area from above. It is usually drawn to *scale*. This means every feature on the map is exactly the right size compared to every other feature on the map. So, if a lake is twice the size of a garden on the ground, the lake will be twice the size of the garden on the map.

There are different kinds of maps. One kind is a *topographic* map. It shows the features of an area of land. A *nautical* map is a map of rivers, lakes, oceans, and coasts. Captains and marine navigators use nautical maps. An *aeronautical* chart shows only large land features that might be seen from the air. Pilots and air navigators use aeronautical charts.

The Goldsteins are looking at a topographic map of the castle grounds. Symbols represent the different features. The pink symbol stands for the castle. The car and letter P show the location of the parking lot. Myra Goldstein is thirsty. Which symbol will show her where the restaurant is?

Picture talk

Point to the spot on the map which shows where the Goldsteins are.

How is the map in the picture different from the area it describes?

Books are great!

Mrs. Vaughan's class is visiting the public library today. Some of the children are looking for books which will give them information on animals. They are working on projects. Others have finished their projects. They are searching for books to take home and read for fun.

Did you know that hundreds of years ago, most people did not know how to read or write? If they wanted to learn about something, they had to find someone who could teach them. Often, as information was passed from person to person, it got mixed up. Communicating exact information by word of mouth was very difficult.

Today, we can learn about any subject from books. Books allow us to keep information without memorizing it. They communicate knowledge and are fun to read. Books are great!

Picture talk

What kinds of books do you like to read? Play the telephone game with ten friends. Think of a message and whisper it to the person sitting next to you. Ask him or her to pass it on to the next person, and so on. Is the message still the same after it has reached the tenth person? What does this game tell you about word-of-mouth information?

Why are books a good source of information?

Sending letters

When people learned to read and write, they started sending letters to one another. We still communicate by writing letters. Sending messages by mail is one of the best ways of keeping in touch.

The Kellys are writing to Grandma Kelly. Brendon will tell her about his hockey game. George has made a greeting card, and baby Olivia is drawing a picture. Mr. and Mrs. Kelly are writing the latest family news.

Mrs. Kelly has just finished addressing her envelope. She will put stamps on it and drop it into a mailbox with the other letters. After all the letters have been mailed, a mail truck will take them to an office where they will be sorted by their *postal codes*.

Grandma's postal code shows the sorters exactly where the letters are going. The letters are then put on a train, boat, or airplane. Finally, they will arrive at the post office nearest Grandma Kelly's house. They will be delivered by a *letter carrier* — right to Grandma's door!

Picture talk

How is writing a good way of communicating? Are all the Kellys using words to communicate to Grandma Kelly? Who is not?
What is Brendon sending to his grandmother in his envelope?

Anna's long-distance call

It is Anna's birthday today. She has just received a present from her grandparents in Australia. Anna wants to call them right away, but her father reminds her that it is the middle of the night there. She waits until the evening to make her call. She lifts the receiver and dials her grandparents.

As Anna speaks into the telephone, a thin metal disk in the mouthpiece vibrates. It sends electricity in short bursts or impulses along the telephone wire. The impulses reach another disk in her grandparents' phone in Australia. The disk vibrates, and Anna's voice comes through!

Anna's grandparents are very happy to hear from their granddaughter. Even though they live so far away, they like to keep in touch by telephone. They call Anna and her family on special occasions such as birthdays. Anna and her parents don't always wait for a special occasion to call. Sometimes they just want to chat!

Anna enjoys writing letters, but she loves speaking with her grandparents by telephone. It makes them seem so much closer.

Picture talk
How old is Anna today?
Name three ways people can communicate birthday wishes.
How often do you make long-distance calls?

Television — a new invention

Imagine you have traveled thirty-five years back in time. Your neighbor, Mr. Chamberlain, has just brought home his very first television set! The Chamberlains invite you to watch a program with them.

The program is in black and white. You ask them to adjust the color. They think you are making a joke! Then you tell them that you have seen this rerun. They laugh again and ask what a rerun is.

The Chamberlains watch program after program. They enjoy a comedy hour. On another show, they learn all about white sharks. Now, it is time for the news. For the first time, the Chamberlains hear and *see* what is happening around the world. You ask them a question. They are not listening. All their attention is on the screen.

Grandma Chamberlain is not happy about the new television. She does not think that having one is a good idea. She remembers the many happy evenings the family used to spend listening to the radio and talking with one another. She wonders about the changes television will bring to their lives. You wonder if she is right.

Picture talk

How is television a good method of communication?
How does it often stop people from communicating in other ways?
Do you think television is a good thing?

Rainbow's concert

"Let's hear it for Rainbow!" Everyone has come to the concert to hear this lively group. Ricky Rain is the leader of the band. He is the main singer. He also plays the electric guitar.

Ricky's song is about summer. He communicates his feelings about summer through his music. He sings songs about other things, too. One of his best-selling records is about a dog named Pizza.

Ricky sings his songs into the microphone. The microphone picks up the sound and sends it to the speakers. Everyone hears Ricky's voice through the large speakers at the sides of the stage. Some of Rainbow's instruments are plugged into *amplifiers*. The amplifiers also carry the sound to the speakers. Rainbow's music can be heard for blocks!

The people in the audience like Ricky's songs. They enjoy Rainbow's lively beat. They dance, sing, wave, and clap to show that they are having a good time.

Picture talk

Where do you hear your favorite songs? Do you listen to the radio, tapes, records, or go to concerts?
How do singers communicate their feelings and ideas through songs? Do they sometimes communicate your ideas as well?

News reports

A burglar has just been caught! Can you see him handcuffed to the police officer? Look at all the people crowded around the store. Everyone wants to know what has happened. One boy has even climbed a tree for a better view!

The people who are busy taking pictures and writing down information are *reporters*. They are finding out the details of the attempted burglary. They will soon communicate this information to others.

The woman kneeling in front of the store owner is interviewing him for his version of the story. Part of her interview will be heard on the next radio news report. Behind the interviewer is a photographer. He is taking pictures for the newspaper. The man beside the store owner is a television reporter. He and his assistant are recording the scene on video. Tonight, everyone will see, hear, or read about the burglar.

News reports help us to learn of events quickly and accurately. Without them, we would have to rely on what we hear from other people — or maybe we would all have to climb trees!

Picture talk

Imagine you are a newspaper reporter. What questions would you ask the police officer and the jewelry-store owner?
What kind of reporter would you like to be? Why?

24

An air-traffic-control tower

"Air-traffic-control tower to World Air flight 192. Come in."
"This is World Air 192. Over."
"192, you are cleared for landing."
"Roger, air control."

This is an *air-traffic-control tower*. The people who work here are called *air-traffic controllers*. They use computers and other electronic equipment to communicate with airplanes. Computers give the controllers all the information they need about the take-off and landing schedules. A television screen tells the controllers about weather conditions in the area.

One controller is talking to an airplane pilot through a radio in his headset. He speaks into the microphone and listens for the answer in his earphones. Another is looking at his radar screen. Any aircraft which is flying close to the airport will show up as a bright, moving dot on the screen. The plane's position is recorded, and the controller gives landing instructions. His instructions must be exactly right. In a busy airport, huge jets take off and land one behind the other every two minutes. The controllers must make sure that the airplanes do not crash into one another. Here, communication is a matter of life and death!

Picture talk
What subjects would a person have to study to become an air-traffic controller?
Would you like to do this job? Why?

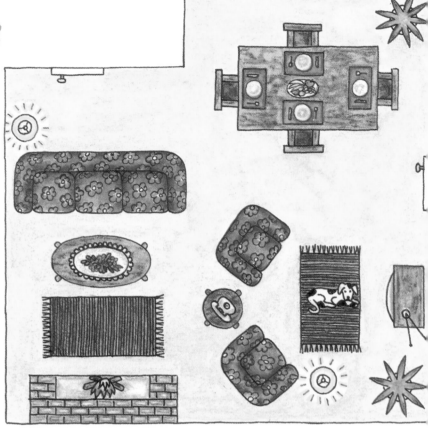

Map-making

Map 1

Pretend you are seeing your living room from above. Look at the shape of your room. Is it a square, a rectangle, or is it L-shaped? What furniture do you have? Is there a sofa and some tables and chairs in your living room? Do you have a television set? Where is the door? How does your furniture look from a bird's-eye view?

Draw your living room and furniture as they would appear from above. Put the furniture in its correct position on the map.

Map 2

Draw a second map of your living room. Instead of drawing your table, think of a symbol or shape for it. It might be a rectangle. Your lamps may be circles, and your table might be an oval. What symbol can you draw for your television set? Draw a *key* such as the one on this page to show what the different symbols on your map mean. When you are finished, make maps of your bedroom, classroom, and playground.

KEY

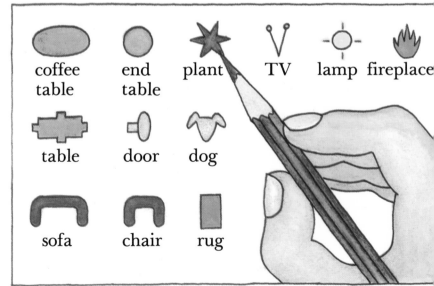

coffee table   end table   plant   TV   lamp   fireplace

table   door   dog

sofa   chair   rug

A map for Aunt Marion

Aunt Marion came to visit last week. After she settled into our guest room and unpacked her suitcases, she was ready to go sightseeing. "My goodness!" she exclaimed, "What a big city. I have a lot of sightseeing to do, but I don't even know where the bus stop is!" "That's no problem," I said. "I'll draw you a map."

I drew a map for Aunt Marion. Then I made a key of all the things on my map. Churches, schools, traffic lights, rivers, and bridges are all important *landmarks* which will help Aunt Marion to find the bus stop.

If you had to help Aunt Marion read my map, what spoken directions would you give her? Do you think she will find the bus stop?

Make a map of your neighborhood

Pretend Aunt Marion is visiting you. Draw a map to show her how to get from your house to the nearest swimming pool or marketplace. Don't forget to include the important landmarks in your neighborhood. Make sure your map is accurate, or Aunt Marion will get lost!

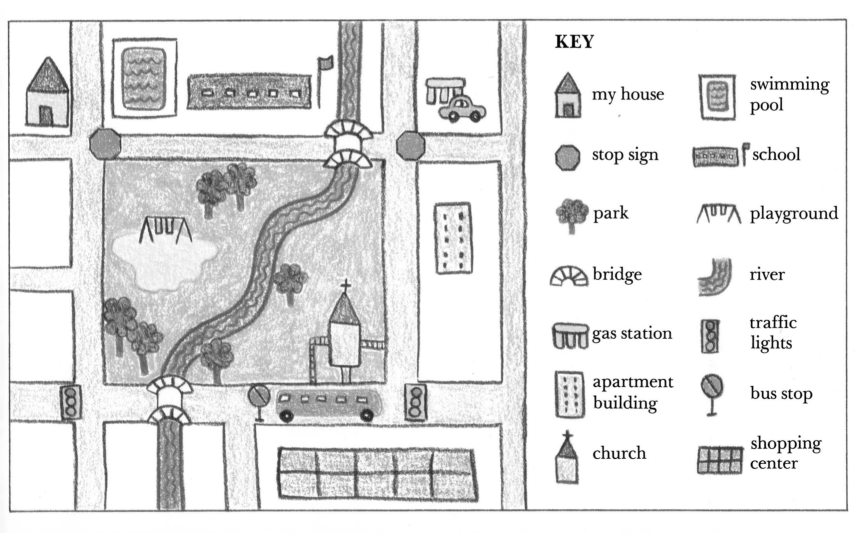

KEY

my house		swimming pool	
stop sign		school	
park		playground	
bridge		river	
gas station		traffic lights	
apartment building		bus stop	
church		shopping center	

Secret codes

Have you ever wanted to send a secret message to a friend? Codes are a good way to disguise messages. Maybe you and your friends can learn one of these codes!

Morse code

In 1838, Samuel Morse developed a code to be used with telegraphs. Combinations of short sounds and long sounds made up different letters of the alphabet. You can turn this sound code into a written code:

A •—   B —•••   C —•—•   D —••   E •   F ••—•

G ——•   H ••••   I ••   J •———   K —•—

L •—••   M ——   N —•   O ———   P •——•

Q ——•—   R •—•   S •••   T —   U ••—

V •••—   W •——   X —••—   Y —•——

Z ——••

The dots and dashes can be written into words. Just put a comma between each letter and a slash between words. Can you read this sentence?

•——, ••••, •—, —/ ••, •••/
—•——, ———, ••—, •—•/
—•, •—, ——, •

It says: "What is your name?" Now, try writing your own sentence. Write, "How are you?" When you are finished, compare it to the correct version in the answer on the next page.

Alphabet code

Here is a secret code that uses the alphabet. Each letter in the alphabet is changed to a different letter.

A – R	N – E
B – I	O – L
C – N	P – Q
D – W	Q – Y
E – C	R – T
F – H	S – X
G – U	T – V
H – Z	U – M
I – O	V – B
J – K	W – J
K – G	X – D
L – A	Y – S
M – P	Z – F

Use the above guide to decode this sentence and then check below for the answer:

B ELC AGC LY ZLYR LY RFN DBCX!

An alphabet system

You can use alphabet systems and vary them from message to message. A simple system is to write the first letter of the alphabet as if it were the fifth, the second as if it were the sixth, and continue this pattern. For example, A is now E, B is F, and C is G. The twenty-second letter will be written as the first letter.

This code can be called "four" because four is the difference in position between the letters in the alphabet and the code letter. How would you write a "six" code?

Answers:
1. How are you?

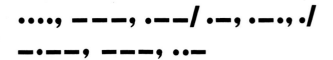

2. I can run as fast as the wind!

Communication dictionary

accurate   Making no mistakes.

air navigator   A person who plans and directs the route of an aircraft.

buoy   A floating object used to mark a dangerous area of water.

communication   The exchange of thoughts, information, and messages.

decode   To translate a code into normal language.

disk   A thin, flat, round object.

distress   Serious danger or trouble.

earphones   Receivers which are held to the ears by a headband.

feature   A part of the landscape that stands out.

flare   A bright light that can be shot into the air as a signal.

gesture   A movement of a part of the body which expresses a feeling or idea.

history   The story or record of what has happened in the past.

island   A piece of land on the road completely surrounded by pavement.

key   A list or chart that explains the symbols, codes, or abbreviations used in maps.

landmark   A feature in the landscape that serves as a guide.

letter carrier   A person who delivers the mail from house to house.

marine navigator   A person who directs and plans the route of a boat.

mouthpiece   The part of the telephone receiver that is held to the mouth.

navigate   To direct and plan a route for a boat or aircraft.

occupant   A person who fills a position or lives in a place.

receiver   The part of the telephone used for listening and speaking.

reporter   A person who gathers or reports news for a television station, newspaper, or radio station.

roger   Message understood.

sign   A board or poster that gives information or points something out.

signal   A sign or action that causes another action.

surroundings   The things that are around or near a person.

symbol   Something that represents something else.

texture   The feel of an object.

vibrate   To move back and forth very quickly.

word of mouth   Communicating by speaking.

123456789 BP Printed in Canada 543210987

Northpoint Elementary IMC
50800 Cherry Rd.
Granger, IN 46530